DEMCO

THE CHEROKEES

A First Americans Book

Virginia Driving Hawk Sneve

illustrated by Ronald Himler

Holiday House/New York

Library of Congress Cataloging-in-Publication Data
Sneve, Virginia Driving Hawk.
The Cherokees / Virginia Driving Hawk Sneve ; illustrated by
Ronald Himler. — 1st ed.
p.   cm. — (A First Americans book)
Includes index.
Summary: Discusses the history, culture, and present situation of
the Cherokees.
ISBN 0-8234-1214-8 (alk. paper)
1. Cherokee Indians — Juvenile literature. [1. Cherokee Indians.
2. Indians of North America.]   I. Himler, Ronald, ill.   II. Title.
III. Series: Sneve, Virginia Driving Hawk. First Americans book.
E99.C5S645   1996   95-24099   CIP   AC
973'.04975 — dc20

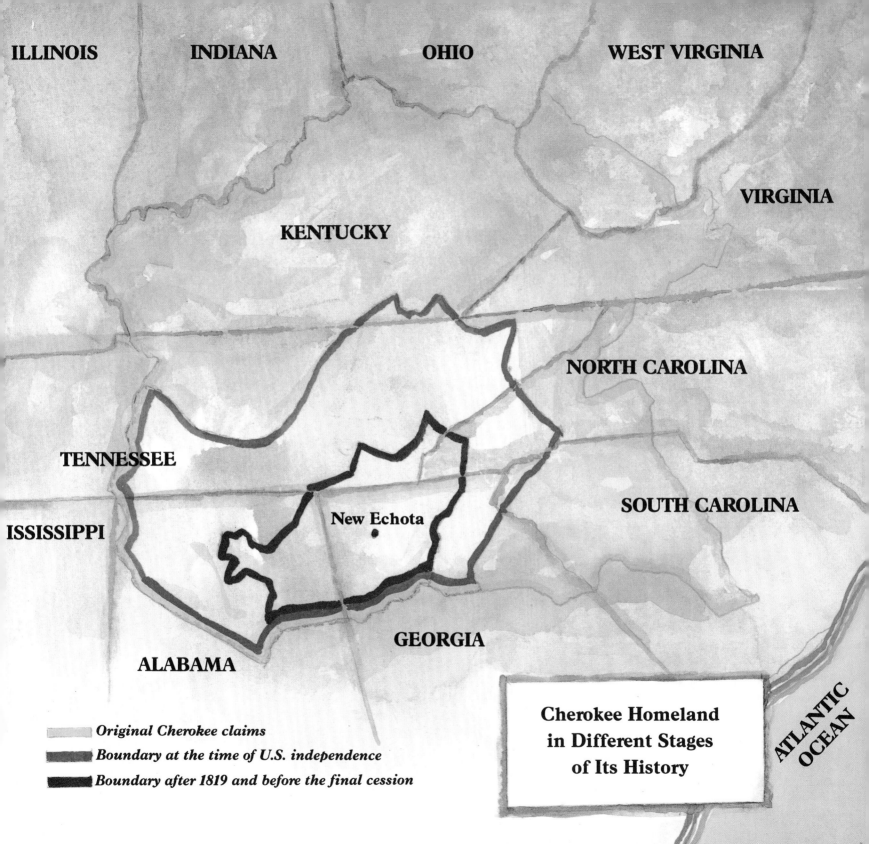

ILLINOIS

INDIANA

OHIO

WEST VIRGINIA

VIRGINIA

KENTUCKY

NORTH CAROLINA

TENNESSEE

SOUTH CAROLINA

ISSISSIPPI

New Echota

ALABAMA

GEORGIA

ATLANTIC OCEAN

Original Cherokee claims

Boundary at the time of U.S. independence

Boundary after 1819 and before the final cession

Cherokee Homeland in Different Stages of Its History

CREATION STORY

Rattlesnake, bear, and owl show this man the center,
where their voices rise as smoke from blue mountain.
GLADYS CARDIFF

Once the world was covered with water. The animals lived in a large rocky place under the arch of the sky. They were so crowded, several of them worried that they would be pushed out of the sky. The animals called a council. They looked at the water below and asked, "Can we live down there?"

A little Water Beetle said, "I will find out."

The beetle left the rocky place and darted over the water. He couldn't find any place to rest. He dove deep into the sea and came up with a tiny bit of mud. The mud grew until it became the earth. It was held in place by strong ropes that stretched from its four corners to the arch in the sky.

Next the animals sent the Great Buzzard to see if the new soil was firm. The buzzard flew over the mud. Wherever his giant wings struck the earth, a valley was formed. Wherever his wings swooped up, a mountain was made.

After the earth was dry, the animals came down from the arch. Human beings appeared on the earth. The first man was *Kanati*, "Lucky Hunter." The first woman was *Selu*, "Corn." They were called the *Ani Yunwiya*, which means "Real" or "Principal" people. They lived in the center of the earth.

HOMELAND

**winter house
(cutaway view)**

summer house

The Ani Yunwiya came to be known as the Cherokees. The name might have been changed by white men from *'tciloki*, a southeastern Indian word meaning "people of a different speech."

The Cherokees once lived in the mountain areas of what are now the states of Virginia, West Virginia, parts of North and South Carolina, Kentucky, Tennessee, Georgia, and Alabama.

The tribe was made up of seven clans, groups of people descended from the same person.

The Cherokees lived in towns with thirty to sixty houses. The most important, the Town House, was built in the center next to a square. The square was used for dances, games, and ceremonies. It was surrounded by all the Cherokee homes.

The Cherokees lived in two kinds of houses. Their summer homes were oblong. They were made of logs, plastered with clay inside and out, and shingled with tree bark. The summer houses were divided into three large rooms with connecting doors.

interior of council house

The winter houses were round with cone-shaped thatched roofs. They were warm places with thick walls. A fire burned day and night in the center. Usually families of several relatives lived together.

Each town had its own leader or principal chief. The chief led the town council. Both men and women were allowed to speak in the council. They made decisions that affected all of the people. Once a year a grand council of the towns was held. There was no single chief for all of the Cherokee towns until after the white men came.

MEN

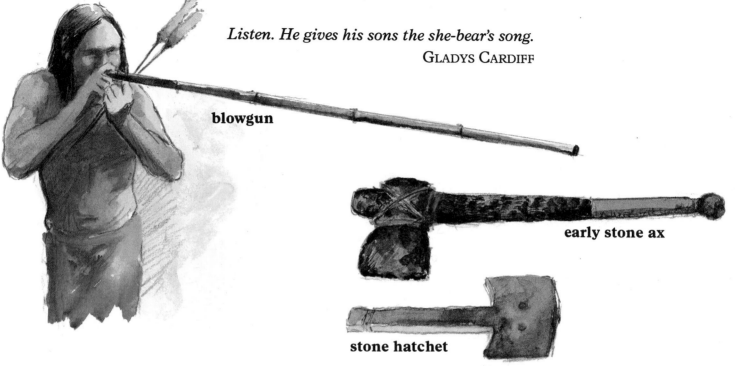

Listen. He gives his sons the she-bear's song.
GLADYS CARDIFF

blowgun

early stone ax

stone hatchet

Cherokee men were warriors of great skill, courage, and daring. The warriors recalled their feats in battle at public meetings. This inspired the young men to be brave warriors, too.

The men wore loincloths and leather moccasins. For special ceremonies, they put on dyed buckskin shirts with matching feather headdresses.

The men cut down trees and cleared fields for planting. They also built houses, made bows, tomahawks, war clubs, and canoes. In addition, they organized the games and ceremonies for the town.

The Cherokees believed that they were a part of nature. It was part of nature's plan for a hunter to kill animals for food. The men used spears, blowguns, and bows and arrows to hunt and fish.

ball sticks

Cherokee men played stickball, a game similar to lacrosse. There were fifty members on a team. Teams from one town played against those of another. The men had to be strong athletes to compete in the rough game. They used a webbed leather basket on a stick to catch a leather-covered ball. Then they threw the ball to the goalpost. Before each game, dances were held in the square to give the players courage.

WOMEN

The tribal tradition recognizes the importance of women.
WILMA MANKILLER

shoulder
bag

Cherokee women had a part in their town's government. They also had their own council headed by a *Ghigau*, or "Beloved Woman." This group discussed issues that went before the town meetings. Each clan selected an "Honored Woman" to attend the yearly gathering of all of the towns.

When it was time for a Cherokee woman to marry, she chose her husband. He built a house for her, or came to her mother's house to live.

Cherokee women owned the children, house, and property. The children became members of their mother's clan.

The women wore apron-type leather skirts. After the white men arrived, the women wore cotton skirts and jackets trimmed with lace and beads. They wore leather leggings and moccasins.

pack basket

river cane basket

Women planted the crops, cared for the livestock, smoked the meat, tanned the hides, and made and repaired the clothing. They also wove baskets, rugs, and mats. They tended their houses and cared for the children, carrying them in cradleboards until they were old enough to walk.

Some women were also warriors. They were known as War Women or Pretty Women.

CHILDREN

Preparing hair. Something women do for each other,
plaiting the generations.

GLADYS CARDIFF

Boys and girls learned Cherokee history and traditions by listening to the stories told by the elders during ceremonies.

As soon as the children were old enough to understand, they were taught to ignore hunger and pain. They were expected to be polite to adults. All children learned to respect the earth and its animals.

Young children did not wear much clothing, unless they were cold, until age eleven, when they began to dress like adults.

Boys and girls played together until age ten. After that, boys joined the company of older boys and men.

A boy learned how to hunt, be a warrior, and about ceremonies from his mother's brothers. Boys were eager to be warriors and hunters.

The girls were always near other females. A girl learned household duties by watching and helping her mother and her mother's sisters. She did errands for her mother and helped care for her younger brothers and sisters. She assisted with weaving, making baskets, and gardening.

CEREMONY AND DANCE

. . . as long as the Cherokees continue traditional dances, the world will remain as it is, but when the dances stop, the world will come to an end.

WILMA MANKILLER

water drum

black buffalo dance mask

gourd rattle

The Cherokees believed that the world had to be kept in balance. They tried always to behave correctly so that their lives would be good. They had ceremonies to help keep harmony on earth.

The most important was the Green Corn Ceremony. It was held when the corn ripened. This marked the end of an old year and the beginning of a new one.

At the start of the green corn rite, the sacred flame in the Town House was allowed to die. All fires were put out in every home. Then the *Adawehis*, or medicine man, lit a new sacred blaze in the square. A torch was lit from the new fire and carried to restart household fires.

The women got rid of old clothing and household furnishings. They cleaned their homes and the Town House. Every person bathed in a stream. The adults sipped the black drink. This made them vomit to get rid of the bad things inside the body. All crimes except murder were forgiven.

At night, the Cherokees held stomp dances. The women wore leg rattles made of pebble-filled turtle shells. They stamped their feet in time to drumbeats to make the shells rattle. The dances celebrated a new beginning of Cherokee life for the next year.

The Cherokees believed that they should say a prayer before killing an animal. If this was not done, the hunters might get sick. Special dances and ceremonies were held before hunting. The Buffalo Hunt Dance was performed by men and women wearing buffalo masks. In the late fall, the Bear Dance took place. The dances showed respect for the animals and thanked them for giving up their lives to feed the people.

The Cherokees had healers who used plants and herbs as medicine to help the sick. They believed that the plants' spirits gave themselves to cure human ills.

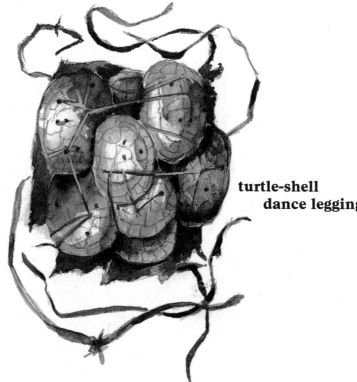

turtle-shell dance leggings

Green Corn dance

THE COMING OF THE WHITE MEN

When the white men came, and some Cherokees took on new ways, their world became unbalanced and bad things happened.

WILMA MANKILLER

Stalking Turkey (Cunne Shote), Cherokee chief and warrior

In 1540 the Cherokees met Hernando de Soto, the Spaniard who explored the Southeast. On and off for the next hundred years, English colonists came to the seacoast. In 1684 England made a treaty with the Cherokees as a sovereign nation, or a country that ruled itself. Later the United States also recognized the Cherokee Nation in treaties. But after each treaty, the Cherokees lost more land.

In 1738 ships brought smallpox to South Carolina. It spread among all of the Cherokees. Almost half of the people died in one year. The disease killed more Cherokees in 1759. The white men also brought measles which killed children as well as adults.

In 1754 the French and English fought for land in North America. The Cherokees sided with the English. After the war, the Cherokees signed a treaty with England. In 1775 the Cherokees sold land to white men. This area later became the state of Kentucky.

During the American Revolutionary War (1775–1783), the Cherokees helped the English fight the Americans. But the English did not protect Cherokee towns.

More than fifty towns were destroyed and hundreds of warriors were killed. On May 20, 1777, the Cherokees signed their first treaty with South Carolina. They had to move out of the state because white settlers wanted their land. In 1785 the Cherokees signed a treaty with the U.S. government and the Indians lost more land. By 1819 the Cherokees had lost about 75 percent of what they'd originally owned.

The Cherokees were angry because their land kept shrinking. The people could no longer depend on hunting for food. They had to rely on farming. They raised cattle and hogs which they had gotten from the white men.

Over the years, white traders had come to the Cherokee Nation. A number of them married Cherokee women. These men were protected by the tribe and helped their wives farm. By 1800 there were many people of mixed blood.

The mixed bloods were at home in the white world. They also got along with their Indian relatives. They and their families lived like rich southern planters. A few of the mixed-blood men became leaders of the Cherokee Nation.

SEQUOYA'S ALPHABET

What I have done I have done from myself.
SEQUOYA

Sequoya

In 1801 German missionaries tried to convert many Cherokees to Christianity, without success. Later, Baptist missionaries reported hundreds of converts. They supplied teachers to schools built by the Cherokees. However, not all of the Indians learned to read and write English.

In 1821 Sequoya, a mixed blood, developed a Cherokee alphabet. Now it was possible for all of the tribe to read and write in their own language.

On February 21, 1828, the *Cherokee Phoenix*, a weekly newspaper, was started in the Cherokee capital of New Echota, Georgia. Elias Boudinot was the editor. It was printed half in English and half in Sequoya's alphabet. It was the first Native American newspaper.

The Cherokee Nation owned the printing press. Besides the newspaper, the people printed church pamphlets and hymnbooks in the Cherokee language.

A GREAT CHANGE

You asked us to throw off the hunter and warrior state . . .
you asked us to form a republican government. We did so . . .

JOHN RIDGE

John Ross

Major Ridge

A number of Cherokees believed that they had to change in order to save what land was left. Thomas Jefferson encouraged the Cherokees to live like white men. In 1809 they set up a central government that acted for the whole tribe.

Some Cherokees liked living as white men. Others hated it because of the great changes. A man could no longer be a warrior or provide for his family by hunting. Women could no longer speak in meetings. Property no longer belonged to women.

In 1802 the U.S. government, hungry for land, signed an agreement with Georgia. The U.S. government urged the Cherokees to exchange their homeland for land in the West. But only a few Cherokees agreed. The rest refused.

In 1828 a mixed blood, John Ross, was elected principal chief. In that year gold was discovered on Cherokee land in Georgia. In 1829 Andrew Jackson, now president of the United States, told the U.S. Congress that the Indians of the Southeast had to be removed to Indian Territory west of the Mississippi River. He said, "Build a fire under them. When it gets hot enough, they'll move."

Ten days later, the state of Georgia passed laws which ended the Cherokees' self-government. Now the Cherokee Nation was under state control, but the Indians were not protected by Georgia laws. They were not allowed to look for gold, yet white gold seekers kept moving into Cherokee lands.

In 1830 Congress passed the Indian Removal Act to force the Cherokees and other southeastern tribes to move west. Chief John Ross and a few U.S. citizens tried to stop approval of the law, but could not.

Major John Ridge, a mixed blood, was the leader of a group of Cherokees who were afraid that Georgia would take their lands away without any payment. On December 29, 1835, Major Ridge and a few hundred Cherokees signed a treaty with the U.S. government. They agreed to move in return for 5 million dollars and 13 million acres in the West. This was called the Treaty of New Echota. Ridge and the men who signed it came to be known as the Treaty Party.

Almost 16,000 other Cherokees did not want the treaty. They were called the Ross Party because they signed a petition that John Ross took to Washington. But President Jackson did not even look at the paper. He no longer recognized the government of the Cherokee Nation.

On May 23, 1836, Congress approved the New Echota Treaty.

TRAIL OF TEARS

And if you send the whole nation, the whole nation will die.
We ask pity.

From A Cherokee Petition

In May 1838 General Winfield Scott sent troops into the Cherokee Nation to round up the Indians. The people were removed from their homes. Their weapons were taken away. They only took what food, clothing, or cooking pots they could carry in their arms. They were forced to march to stockades or prisons. They stayed there until they were sent west.

From 1838 to 1839, about 17,000 Cherokees left their homelands. They traveled in seventeen different groups. Some of them went in boats on the Tennessee and Mississippi rivers and as far as they could go on the Arkansas. After that they walked to Indian Territory.

The other groups traveled overland through Tennessee, Illinois, Missouri, or Arkansas. A few of them rode in wagons or on horseback, but most had to walk.

It was a terrible journey for all of the Cherokees. They suffered in the heat of summer or the cold of winter. They trudged through dust and mud. Babies were born on the way, and the mother and child often got lost. All of the people were hungry and many got sick.

Every day children, mothers, fathers, and grandparents were buried. Four thousand Cherokees died either in the stockades, on the boats, or on the trail west. The Cherokees called the dreadful trip, "The Trail Where We Cried."

EASTERN CHEROKEES

These hills are Cherokee, and Cherokees slip into their brambles and their brush like a fish glides through a stream.

Robert J. Conley

TENNESSEE

Great Smoky Mountains

Qualla Boundary

NORTH CAROLINA

Tsali

Not all of the Cherokees were rounded up. About four hundred of the Qualla band lived in North Carolina on their own land. They did not have to move.

Other of the Cherokees avoided being rounded up or escaped before they reached the stockades. Several hundred hid in North Carolina's caves and mountains.

Among this group was a man named Tsali or Charley. Tsali was accused of killing two soldiers. Tsali agreed to give himself up if the rest of the hidden Cherokees would be allowed to stay in North Carolina. Tsali, his sons, and a son-in-law were captured and killed.

The Cherokees came out of hiding and were not sent west, but they had no homes. William Thomas, the adopted son of a Cherokee chief, bought mountain lands for the homeless Cherokees. This area and the lands of the Qualla band became known as the Qualla Boundary. In 1866 North Carolina recognized the Cherokees as permanent residents of the state.

Cherokees in Alabama and Tennessee who lived outside the Cherokee Nation boundaries were not moved west.

WESTERN CHEROKEES

A Cherokee can disappear from white men's eyes
in the wooded hills of Oklahoma.

ROBERT J. CONLEY

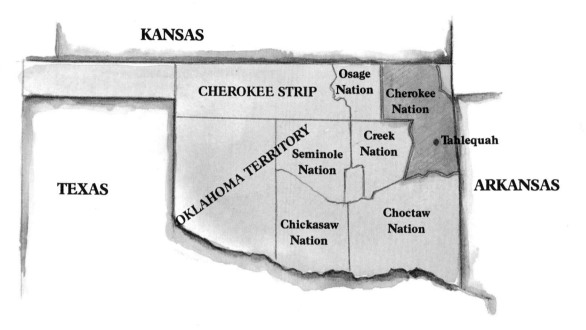

The Cherokees' new home was in Indian Territory in what became the state of Oklahoma. The Cherokees were divided into three parties: the Old Settlers or Westerners (who had moved before the treaty of 1835), the Treaty Party (who had signed the New Echota Treaty and agreed to move west), and the Ross Party (who had opposed the treaty and the move west). They disagreed on several issues, but in 1839 John Ross was elected principal chief.

The Cherokee Nation began again. It had a new government with its capital at Tahlequah. The Cherokees started businesses, ranches, and farms. They built schools and churches.

The Western Cherokees were doing well in their new home when the Civil War began. It was fought between Northern and Southern states. The North wanted to rid the nation of slavery; the South wanted slavery to remain. Some of the Cherokees who owned slaves wanted to join the South. Others supported the Northern cause. Another group did not want to fight at all even though the Southern states had treated the Cherokees badly. Two Cherokee regiments were formed under Southern command. They were defeated at the Battle of Pea Ridge in March 1862. There was also fighting among the Cherokees and many were killed.

After the Civil War, the Cherokees gave up more than 6 million acres to the United States. This was known as the Cherokee Outlet or Cherokee Strip. The area was supposed to be used for new homes for other Native American tribes who would be moved to Indian Territory, but instead, it was opened to white settlers.

In 1887 under the U.S. General Allotment Act, the Cherokee country was divided by the government. Each tribal member was assigned a parcel of land. The leftover areas were opened to homesteaders. In 1893 more than one hundred thousand white settlers raced into the Cherokee Strip to stake claims.

The U.S. Congress ended the Cherokee Nation's government in 1898. It did away with tribal laws and courts. Now the Cherokees' chief would be appointed by the president of the United States.

In 1907 Indian Territory became the state of Oklahoma.

The Cherokees hated the way the U.S. government was again forcing changes upon the tribe. They were sad at how helpless they had become. Many of them showed their support for the Cherokee Nation by joining the Keetoowah Society.

The Keetoowah were Cherokees who had always resisted the white men's ways. After the move west, the society kept the traditional ceremonies alive. They were also called Nighthawks because they met secretly at night. They were the keepers of the Cherokees' sacred fire.

TODAY

I know who I am, what I am, and what I can do or cannot do. I am a Cherokee and I am proud of it. There is no one who can take that away from me.

CHARLIE SOAP

seal of the Cherokee Nation

In 1971 the U.S. government let the Cherokees choose their own chief. W. W. Keeler was elected principal chief.

Today Cherokees are employed as farmers, ranchers, doctors, lawyers, teachers, and in other professional occupations. There are artists, writers, and musicians that keep the Cherokees' heritage alive through their creative work.

The Eastern Cherokee Reservation has its headquarters in Cherokee, North Carolina. A pageant, *Unto These Hills,* shows the Cherokees' history during summer nights.

Near Calhoun, Georgia, the New Echota State Historic Site is located. It is the original capital of the Cherokee Nation. The Cherokee Nation of Oklahoma has no reservation. Its members live in fourteen counties in northeastern Oklahoma. The tribal government is still at Tahlequah, where the drama *Trail of Tears* is presented in an open-air theater.

In 1984 the Oklahoma Cherokees and the Eastern Band of Cherokees had a reunion at Red Clay, Tennessee. It was the first meeting of the two groups since the 1838 removal. They played a stickball game and held traditional dances. A torch was set ablaze at Cherokee, North Carolina. Runners carried the flame 150 miles to Red Clay. There the sacred fire of the Cherokees was lit.

In 1985 Wilma Mankiller was elected principal chief of the Oklahoma Cherokee Nation. She was the first woman to lead all of the Western Cherokees. Joe Byrd was elected in 1995, ending Ms. Mankiller's ten years of service.

We are now about to take our leave and kind farewell to our native land, the country that the great spirit gave our Fathers; we are on the eve of leaving that country that gave us birth . . . it is with sorrow that we are forced by the authority of the white man to quit the scenes of our childhood . . . we bid a final farewell to it and all we hold dear.

GEORGE HICKS, Cherokee Leader,
on the Trail of Tears,
November 4, 1838

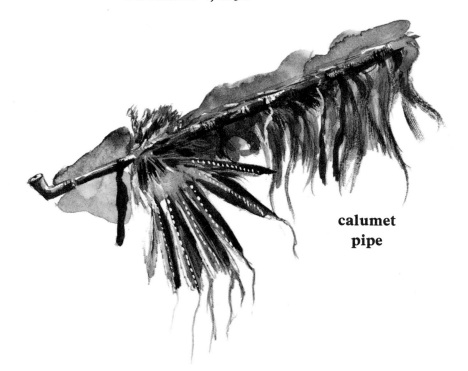

calumet pipe

ACKNOWLEDGMENTS

The Gladys Cardiff selections are from her poems, "Swimmer" and "Combing," from *Carriers of the Dream Wheel*, edited by Duane Niatum, Harper & Row, New York, 1975.

The quotes of Old Tassel, Sequoya, John Ridge, and from a Cherokee petition are from *Trail of Tears: The Rise and Fall of the Cherokee Nation*, by John Ehle, Anchor Books, Doubleday, New York, 1988.

The Robert J. Conley selections are from his poem, "The Hills of *Tsa La Gi*," from *Songs From This Earth on Turtle's Back: Contemporary American Indian Poetry*, edited by Joseph Bruchac, The Greenfield Review Press, Greenfield Center, New York, 1983, reprinted by permission of the author.

The Wilma Mankiller, George Hicks, and Charlie Soap quotations are from *Mankiller: A Chief and Her People*, by Wilma Mankiller and Michael Wallis, St. Martin's Press, New York, NY. Copyright © 1993 by Wilma Mankiller. Reprinted by permission of St. Martin's Press, Inc., New York, NY.

chief's headdress

INDEX